HEROES and HEROINES in music

Wendy-Ann Ensor

Oxford University Press
Music Department, Ely House, 37 Dover Street, London W1X 4AH

SHEHERAZADE

Many years ago there lived a King in the islands near India and China. This King was both brave and strong. For many years he ruled well and all his people loved him.

But after the King had ruled his island for 20 years he was visited by his brother who was King in another country. This brother had a wicked wife. He made the King believe that his wife was wicked too.

Now in those days a King could kill a wicked wife, so the King ordered his wife to be killed. He also thought that if his wife was wicked, all women must be wicked. So he married a new wife each day and then ordered her to be killed the next morning. He did this every day for three years. The people became very frightened and tried to hide their daughters from him.

Now the King had a Wazir (or Wise Man) to carry out his orders and the Wazir had two daughters who were beautiful and clever and wise. The elder daughter had read many books and knew many stories and legends about famous people. When she told a story her voice was like music and everybody wanted to listen to her. The name of the elder daughter was Sheherazade.

Sheherazade's father told her all about the wicked things the King had done and of the great trouble which this had caused in the country. She listened and then asked if she might marry the King. She insisted on being taken to the King. Her father could not change her mind.

When the King saw Sheherazade he was pleased. But she began to cry and said that she could not marry him unless her sister could also come to the palace to be with her. The King agreed and that evening, after they had been married, Sheherazade's sister came and sat beside her. She asked Sheherazade to tell some of her stories so that the King might hear them. Sheherazade had told her sister to do this because she had a plan to save her own life and to stop the King killing his wives.

So Sheherazade began to tell a story to the King and went on until they were all very tired. But the story was not finished. Her sister then told her, as they had planned, how good her story was. Sheherazade said that the best part was still to come and she would finish it if the King let her live until the next night.

The King wanted to hear the end of the story. So Sheherazade continued her story the next night and then another night and continued telling stories night after night. But always when they were tired the King wanted to hear more, and so let her live until the next night.

The stories Sheherazade told were wonderful stories. They were about Sinbad who sailed to many countries, of Ali Baba, of Ala-a-Din, of princes and princesses, of merchants, stories about ordinary people. As the King listened he learned many things. He became wise and no longer wished to kill Sheherazade or any other woman. He began to understand why people do the things they do. He began to love life and people. Sheherazade told her stories for nearly three years for 1,000 nights and one night. By the time she finished her last story she and the King had three children. These stories came to be known as *The Arabian Nights*.

At the end of her last story Sheherazade brought her children to the King and said that he might now kill her as she had come to the end of her stories. But the King now loved Sheherazade. He loved his children and the people of his country. There was no more killing and Sheherazade and the King lived together in happiness for many years. And everybody in that country was happy.

4

The story of Sinbad

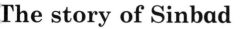

● One of the stories Sheherazade told to the King
was about Sinbad the Sailor.

Once upon a time there was a sailor called Sinbad who
lived in Arabia. One day he set sail for the East Indies
with some merchants.

After a few days they saw an island and decided to
land. But the island moved and suddenly all the sailors
saw it was a whale. The captain managed to rescue
most of the sailors and frighten the whale away. Then
they all sailed away. But one sailor, Sinbad, was left
behind and washed ashore on a lonely island.

As Sinbad looked around he saw a large egg which
was bigger than a man. Suddenly a giant bird flew
down and Sinbad tied the ends of his turban to the
bird's leg so that the bird would carry him with him
when he flew away. The bird flew off with Sinbad, who
was very frightened.

The bird landed in a deep valley which was full of
diamonds. Night came and large snakes crawled
around the rocks. Poor Sinbad was very frightened
and hid in a cave.

In the morning Sinbad came out of the cave and
collected some of the diamonds. Near the diamonds he
saw some large lumps of meat. This meat had been
thrown into the valley by merchants. The diamonds
stuck to the meat and were carried by the birds to their
nests. When a bird flew to its nest, the merchants
frightened it away and then took the diamonds.

Sinbad tied the ends of his turban to a large piece of meat and was carried by a bird to its nest. A merchant was waiting at the nest and was very surprised to see Sinbad. Sinbad gave the merchant some of the diamonds and the merchant helped him to find his way home. Sinbad's wife and family were so happy to see him again.

Sinbad had many more adventures. Once, his ship lost its way in a great storm. The waves crashed over the ship and flung it against the rocks of an island. The ship was split in two and all the sailors were killed except Sinbad who swam to the land. Sinbad explored the island and after more adventures found his way home.

About the music

The story of Sinbad is one of the *Arabian Nights* stories that Sheherazade told the King to stop him from killing her.

In the year 1889, a Russian composer called Nicholas Rimsky-Korsakov wrote a suite (or set of pieces) which he called *Sheherazade*. It was based on some of the stories which Sheherazade told and is divided into four parts or 'movements'. Here are some ideas about each movement.

First movement

The music first shows you the King who is a sad and dangerous man. Then a violin plays on its own. This is Sheherazade telling the story of Sinbad. You can hear Sinbad's ship rocking on the sea.

● Have you ever been on a boat on the sea or on a river? Divide into two groups. Group 1 take bells, shakers and tambourines. Choose one person to play the chime bars.

Now Group 1 should shake its instruments gently to sound like the sea rocking Sinbad's ship. Play the chime bars gently to sound like the waves against the side of the ship. While Group 1 are making rocking music for Sinbad's ship, Group 2 could sit on the floor, each person with a partner. Face your partner and hold hands. Now rock backwards and forwards to the music like a ship on the sea.

Next time the movement is played Group 1 can be the ships and Group 2 play the instruments.

Second movement

Sheherazade now tells of a prince pretending to be a holy man. Listen to him go on his travels and then hear him tell the King of a battle. Listen to the trumpets. Who do you think won the battle?

- Use your two groups again. Group 1 could use the cymbals, clappers, drums and tambourines to make battle music. Group 2 could roll pieces of paper into a cone shape and then make a trumpet sound by blowing into them.

Now put your instruments down and be the horses galloping round the battlefield.

Third movement

In the third story Sheherazade tells of a young prince who refuses to marry but then falls in love with a beautiful princess from another country.

- Listen to her dance. Can you make up a dance for a happy princess to this music? Use the bells and tambourines to play with the music. Use your arms and hands as well as your legs and feet when you are dancing.

Now find some material, braid, net and sequins. Make a picture of a dancing princess like the one in the photograph.

Fourth movement

In the last movement, Sheherazade tells of a Festival at Baghdad. There is a procession and dancing.

● Take a tambourine, drum, bells, triangles or shakers and join the procession. Tap or shake your instrument gently so you can hear the music. You can walk or dance in the procession.

Then the music changes as the King remembers the story of Sinbad.

● Listen to the storm at sea. Some of you use the shakers, tambourines and drums to make stormy music. You can hear the waves crashing against the ship. Others take partners, sit down and make your boats again to be Sinbad's ship in the storm.

At the end, the music shows the King no longer angry. Sheherazade has made him understand through her stories. Her music is combined with his.

● Dance by yourself or with a partner to this music to show that you will live happily ever after.

Read some of the exciting stories from the Arabian Nights. They are full of adventures, robbers, treasure, cruel men and beautiful girls. You have read the story of Sinbad in this book. See if you can find Aladdin and Ali Baba in your library. These stories all take place in places like Egypt, and Persia.

Mosque

A mosque is a place of worship in the East. Many mosques have beautiful carvings and decorations. These decorations are made of mosaics. Mosaic is a pattern made with small coloured pieces of stone or glass.

Make your own mosque, like this one.

You will need

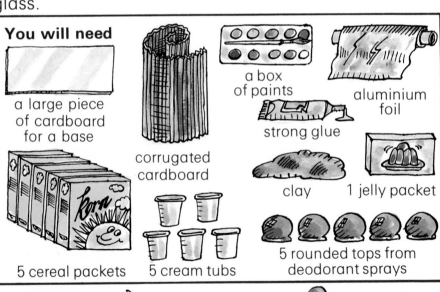

a large piece of cardboard for a base

corrugated cardboard

a box of paints

strong glue

aluminium foil

clay

1 jelly packet

5 cereal packets

5 cream tubs

5 rounded tops from deodorant sprays

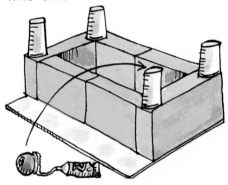

1 Put the base on the table and glue the cereal packets and cream tubs in place. Now glue the rounded tops on the cream tubs.

2 Cut the corrugated cardboard to look like battlements, then glue them on to the cereal packets.

3 Use the jelly packet for a doorway, and make some steps for it with the clay.

4 Paint your mosque. When the paint is dry, cut out windows from the foil and glue them on.

Ali Baba, Morgiana and the Thieves

When you have read the story of Ali Baba and the Forty Thieves, perhaps you could make Ali Baba, some of the thieves and the clever Morgiana who saved Ali Baba's life.

You will need

cord or braid

1 rubber band

1 pipe cleaner

newspaper

1 washing-up liquid bottle

material

glue

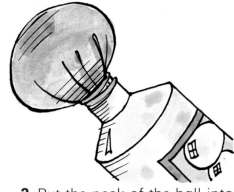

1 Roll the newspaper into a ball and fix a rubber band round the neck.

2 Put the neck of the ball into the top of the bottle.

3 Make a hole in each side of the bottle for the arms and put the pipe cleaner through.

4 Look at the photograph to see how to dress your model. First cover the head with pale pink material.

5 Cut two blue or brown eyes from material and glue on a red mouth and nose.

6 Now glue on some wool for hair. Long hair for Morgiana and shorter hair for Ali Baba and the thieves.

7 *Ali Baba* Cut out two robe shapes. Glue them together and glue on to the body. Choose a piece of material for his headdress and fix with cord or braid. Cut and glue two hands.

8 *Morgiana* Cut out two robe shapes and glue together. Glue on to the body. Cut out and glue on two hands. Choose some thin material for a veil. Make a sash round the waist.

9 *Thief* Cut out two robe shapes. Glue together and glue on to body. Cut out and glue two hands. Tie a sash round his head and fix with a cord or braid.

Clay jars

You could make some jars like the ones the robbers hid themselves in, and put them round the outside of the mosque like the ones in the photograph.

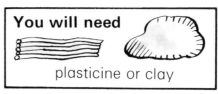

You will need

plasticine or clay

Thumb pot

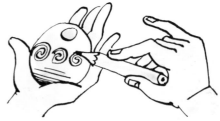

1 Roll a piece of clay or plasticine into a ball. Hold it carefully in one hand and make a hole in the centre with the thumb of your other hand.

2 Turn the ball round and round until your pot is a good shape.

3 Draw patterns on your pot with the point of a pencil.

Coil pot

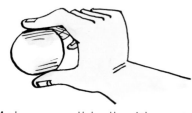

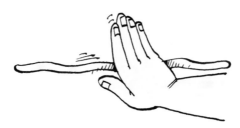

1 Make a small ball with part of the clay or plasticine. Roll it flat and cut or mould into a circle.

2 Take the other piece of clay or plasticine and roll it out into a long snake (coil).

3 Lift one end of the coil and press it round the inside of the clay circle. Keep pressing round and round until you have used up all the coil.

Aladdin's cave

Read the story of Aladdin and his wonderful lamp. His wicked uncle trapped him in a cave full of gold, silver and precious jewels. You can make the cave using a shoe box, and put your models of Ali Baba and the thieves inside it.

You will need

For the cave

a shoebox (or other small open box)

some oil paint

a sheet of plain paper

an oblong baking tray

paints

For the trees

sticky tape

paints

squares of newspaper about 30cm

1 Fill the baking tray with water and splatter some oil paint over it.

2 Blow to spread the paint and lay a sheet of paper over the surface. Take it off carefully and leave to dry.

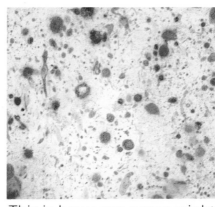

This is how your paper might look when you have blown the oil paint on the water and then put the paper on the surface.

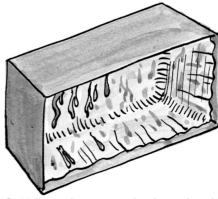

3 When the paper is dry, glue it to the inside of the box and it will look like jewels in the cave.

4 Paint the outside of your cave brown or grey.

5 Make some trees to stand at the door of the cave. Cut the paper halfway down in strips.

6 Roll up the paper, fasten it with sticky tape. Paint the trees brown and green.

Jewellery

Now to make your own jewellery. You will probably find most of the jewels in your school Useful Box.

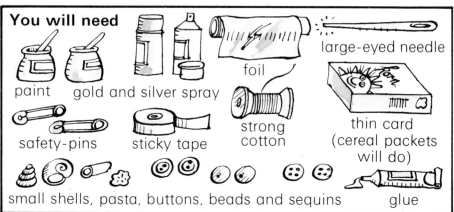

You will need

paint
gold and silver spray
foil
large-eyed needle
safety-pins
sticky tape
strong cotton
thin card (cereal packets will do)
small shells, pasta, buttons, beads and sequins
glue

1 Cut ten squares of foil for beads, roll them into balls until they are round and smooth.

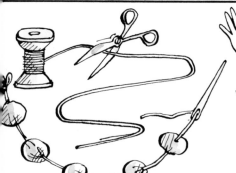

2 Cut a piece of cotton about half a metre long. Thread your needle and push it through five beads. Tie a big knot at both ends of the cotton.

3 Cut another piece the same length and thread the next five beads. Now you have made two bracelets.

4 If you want to make a necklace you will need to make about 25 beads.

5 If you want a change from silver beads, you can paint or spray some of them different colours, or use ordinary beads or pasta shapes instead.

6 To make a brooch, find some buttons, sequins and small shells in the Useful Box. Draw a shape on card and cut it out.

7 Glue the buttons, sequins and shells on to the shape. Spray some of them with gold and silver spray. Fasten a safety-pin on to the back with some sticky tape.

Peter and the Wolf

Early one morning Peter opened the gate and went out into the big green meadow.

On a branch of a big tree sat a little bird, Peter's friend. 'It's a lovely quiet morning', chirped the bird gaily.

Just then a duck came waddling around. She was glad that Peter had not closed the gate, and decided to take a nice swim in the deep pond in the meadow. Seeing the duck, the little bird flew down upon the grass, settled next to her and shrugged his shoulders.

'What kind of bird are you, if you can't fly?' said he. To this the duck replied: 'What kind of bird are you, if you can't swim?' and dived into the pond. They argued and argued, the duck swimming in the pond, the little bird hopping along the shore.

Suddenly, something caught Peter's attention: he saw a cat crawling through the grass. The cat thought: 'The bird is busy arguing. I'll just grab him'. Stealthily she crept towards him on her velvet paws. 'Look out!' shouted Peter, and the bird immediately flew up into the tree. The duck quacked angrily at the cat from the middle of the pond. The cat crawled around the tree and thought: 'Is it worth climbing up so high? By the time I get there, the bird will have flown away.'

Grandfather came out. He was angry because Peter had gone to the meadow. 'It is a dangerous place. If a wolf should come out of the forest, what would you do then?' Peter paid no attention to his Grandfather's words. Boys like him are not afraid of wolves. But Grandfather took Peter by the hand, locked the gate and led him home.

No sooner had Peter gone, than a big grey wolf did come out of the forest. In a flash the cat climbed to the top of the tree. The duck quacked and in her excitement jumped right out of the pond. But no matter how hard the duck tried to run, she couldn't escape the wolf. He was getting nearer – and nearer – catching up with her ... and then he got her, and with one gulp, swallowed her.

And now this is how things stood: the cat was sitting on one branch of the tree, the bird on another – not too close to the cat – and the wolf walked round and round the tree, looking up at them both, with wicked, greedy eyes.

In the meantime, Peter, without the slightest fear, stood behind the closed gate watching all that was going on. He ran home, took a strong rope and climbed up the high stone wall. One of the branches of the tree stretched out over the wall. Grabbing hold of the branch, Peter lightly climbed over into the tree.

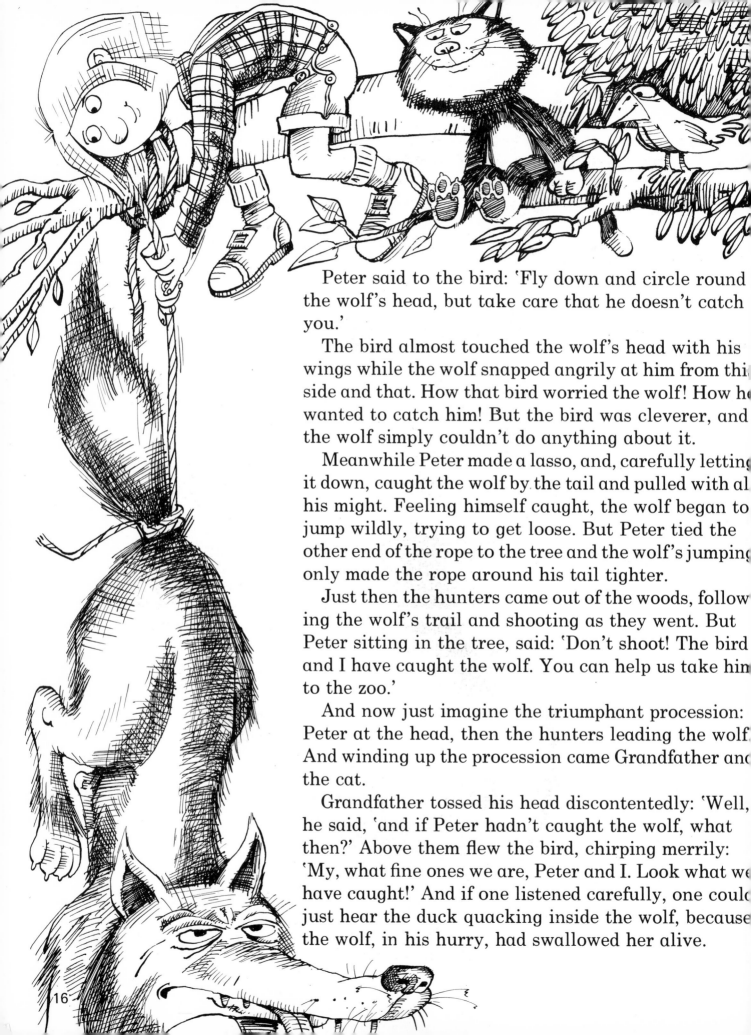

Peter said to the bird: 'Fly down and circle round the wolf's head, but take care that he doesn't catch you.'

The bird almost touched the wolf's head with his wings while the wolf snapped angrily at him from this side and that. How that bird worried the wolf! How he wanted to catch him! But the bird was cleverer, and the wolf simply couldn't do anything about it.

Meanwhile Peter made a lasso, and, carefully letting it down, caught the wolf by the tail and pulled with all his might. Feeling himself caught, the wolf began to jump wildly, trying to get loose. But Peter tied the other end of the rope to the tree and the wolf's jumping only made the rope around his tail tighter.

Just then the hunters came out of the woods, following the wolf's trail and shooting as they went. But Peter sitting in the tree, said: 'Don't shoot! The bird and I have caught the wolf. You can help us take him to the zoo.'

And now just imagine the triumphant procession: Peter at the head, then the hunters leading the wolf. And winding up the procession came Grandfather and the cat.

Grandfather tossed his head discontentedly: 'Well,' he said, 'and if Peter hadn't caught the wolf, what then?' Above them flew the bird, chirping merrily: 'My, what fine ones we are, Peter and I. Look what we have caught!' And if one listened carefully, one could just hear the duck quacking inside the wolf, because the wolf, in his hurry, had swallowed her alive.

About the music

This music was written by the Russian composer Serge Prokofiev, who died in the early 1950s. He wrote the story too. Listen to how the story is told by the instruments of the orchestra as well as words.

The **bird**, who chirps merrily, is played by the flute.

The **duck**, swimming, arguing and frightened, is played by the oboe.

Peter, who is a bright and cheerful boy, is played by the violins.

The **cat**, slinking along, is played by the clarinet.

Grandfather, slow and plodding, is played by the bassoon.

The **wolf**, prowling round and round, is played by the French horns.

The **huntsmen** are played by the kettle drums and a bass drum; you will hear them fire their guns.

More about the instruments of the orchestra

The orchestra is made up of four families of instruments. These are the strings, woodwind, brass and percussion. The woodwind and brass are wind instruments but the woodwind, except for some flutes, are made of wood and the brass instruments are made of brass. The brass instruments are louder than woodwind instruments, and more powerful. In *Peter and the Wolf* there are some instruments from each of these sections.

Violin – Strings

This is the smallest member of the string family. One hand holds the narrow end, while the chin rest tucks under the player's chin. This leaves the other hand free to hold the bow and draw it across the four strings. These strings vibrate through the bridge and over the sound box, which makes the notes. The strings may also be plucked by the fingers without using the bow.

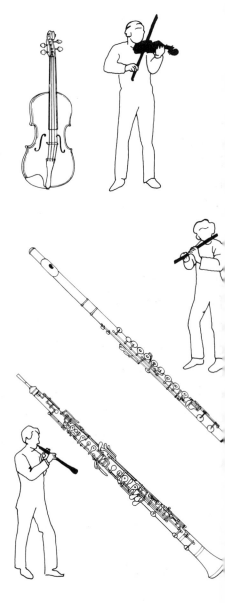

Flute – Woodwind

This is a pipe made of wood or metal and has a mouthpiece in the side. The player puts his mouth over this blow-hole and can make high sweet notes like the bird.

Oboe – Woodwind

This is a double reed instrument – that is, it has two reeds with which to blow through the mouthpiece. To make the reed a short piece of cane is split into three pieces. These pieces are then bent over and bound to a piece of metal. The tips are cut very thin to make them vibrate.

Bassoon – Woodwind

This is a *bass* wind instrument – that is, it is the lowest sounding wind instrument of the orchestra. It has a deep, rich sound like grandfather. The bassoon has a double reed like the oboe.

Clarinet – Woodwind

This is a single reed instrument – that is, it has one reed, usually made of cane but sometimes of plastic. The reed is fixed to the mouthpiece and the player blows into it. The music can sound tender and loving or fierce and soldier-like. This instrument is ideal for the slinky cat stalking the duck.

French horn – Brass

This is really a long narrow tube made of brass which is curled, or coiled, up. The player presses his lips against the cupped mouthpiece and blows. One hand holds the horn near the mouthpiece and the other hand is placed in the bell to support the horn. Three French horns play the music of the wolf.

Kettledrum – Percussion

Drums are found in the percussion section of the orchestra, and they play a very important part. Kettledrums were played in Ancient Egypt, and today they are played in America, Africa, Asia and the countries of Europe. In *Peter and the Wolf* the kettledrums and the bass drums play the huntsmen's music and if you listen carefully you can hear them fire their guns.

Bass drum – Percussion

The bass drum is usually played with two wooden sticks which have padded ends.

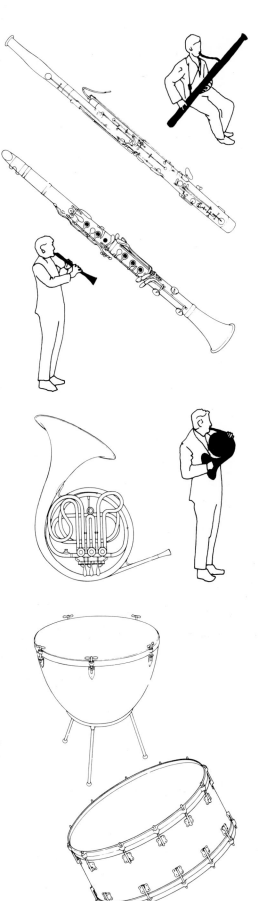

Here is a song about the instruments played in *Peter and the Wolf*. You can sing the song and do actions to it.

Oh, we can play on the big bass drum

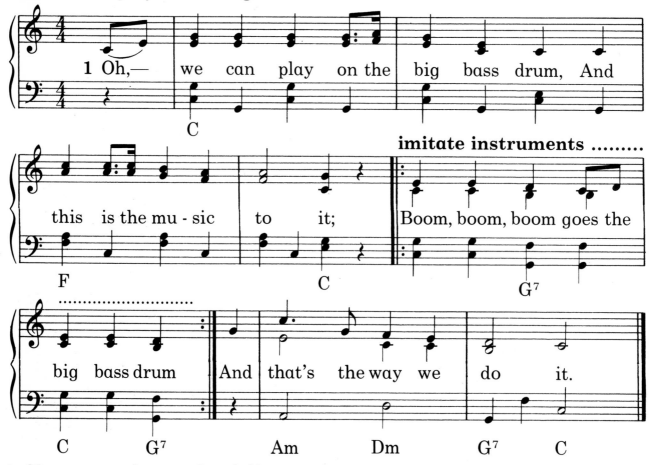

2 Oh, we can play on the violin,
And this is the music to it;
Fiddle, fiddle, fiddle goes the violin;
Boom, boom, boom goes the big bass drum,
And that's the way we do it.

3 Oh, we can play on the whistling flute,
Chirp, chirp, chirp goes the whistling flute,
Fiddle, fiddle, fiddle goes the violin, etc.

4 Oh, we can play on the big bassoon,
Broom, broom, broom goes the big bassoon.

5 Oh, we can play on the brass French horn,
Daa-diddle-daa goes the brass French horn.

Things to do and make

Musical instruments

You can make your own musical instruments.

String instruments

First a stringed instrument like a violin.

a box
(a shoebox
will do)

8 different
size rubber
bands

1 Stretch the rubber bands round a shoebox.

2 Try plucking them and see if you can make some sounds like the violins in the story.

Wind instruments

The flute, clarinet, oboe, bassoon and horns all produce music when they are blown into. Try your own wind instruments.

You will need 6 bottles, all different shapes and sizes.

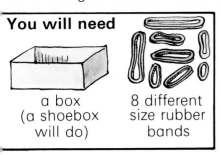

1 Blow into the bottles. You will be able to make some sounds.

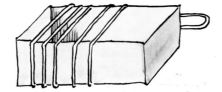

2 Now partly fill some of the bottles with water and blow over them carefully. You should get *different* sounds.

3 Now hit them with a stick. Do they sound different when they have different amounts of water in them?

Drum

The huntsmen's music was made by kettledrums and the bass drum. Try and make your own drums.

You will need

a large coffee tin
or a saucepan

some
paper

1 Fix the paper tightly over the tin or pan with an elastic band or sellotape.

2 Tap gently. Put the lid on the tin. Does it make a different sound?

When you next listen to the music, you can join in with your own musical instruments.

Listen again to the tape or record and this time see if you can act the brave Peter or the slinky cat or perhaps even the cunning wolf.

The wolf in the story was a clever, cunning animal. Can you find other stories with wolves in them? Read *The Wolf and the Seven Little Kids*.

Make models of the characters in *Peter and the Wolf* and then they can act the story to the music.

Peter, Grandfather and the huntsmen

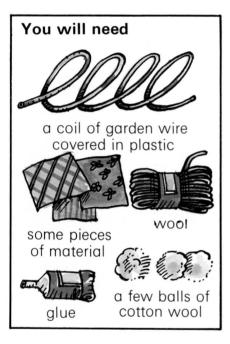

You will need

a coil of garden wire covered in plastic

some pieces of material

wool

glue

a few balls of cotton wool

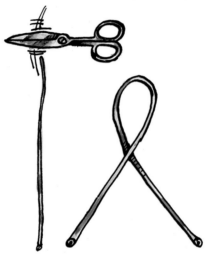

1 Cut a piece of wire about 30cm long, fold it in two and twist a round piece for the head.

2 Then twist it twice for the neck, inserting another piece about 12cm long for the arms.

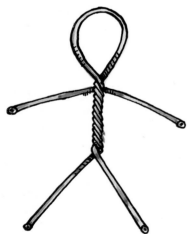

3 Continue twisting the wire for the body, then divide for the legs.

4 Now cover the wire in a light-coloured material.

5 Cut out and glue on eyes, nose, mouth and the wool for hair.

6 Dress Peter. Cut out a shirt and a pair of trousers. Glue carefully on to the wire body.

7 Do not forget to use white wool or cotton wool for Grandfather's hair, moustache and beard.

8 Make the huntsmen's hats from sections of an egg box. Paint them and glue a small feather on the side.

The bird

Now you are ready to make Peter's friend, the bird.

You will need

cotton wool balls

a sheet of cardboard

paints or felt tips

1 Glue two cotton wool balls together.

2 Draw a beak, two eyes, two wings and two feet on cardboard.

3 Paint the eyes blue, the beak and feet red, and the wings yellow.

4 Glue the eyes and beak on to the bird's head.

5 Glue the wings and feet on to its body. Now your bird is ready.

AIDA

Three thousand years ago, in a country in North Africa called Egypt, there lived a slave girl called Aida (pronounced I-ee-da). She was really a princess, the daughter of the King of Ethiopia, but had been captured by the Egyptian soldiers who did not know her father was the King. So she was brought to Egypt and became the slave of the King of Egypt's daughter, the Princess Amneris.

Now Aida loved a General of Egypt called Radames (Rad-am-es) and he loved her. But unfortunately Radames was also loved by the Princess Amneris.

One day an army from Ethiopia entered Egypt. The King asked his General Radames to defend Egypt and defeat the army of Ethiopia which was led by the King of that country. Now Aida knew that the King of Ethiopia was her father but she told no one her secret. She prayed to the gods to show her whether she should hope for the death of Radames whom she loved, or for the defeat of her country and the death of her father.

Radames won the battle and returned in triumph to Egypt with many prisoners and much treasure. The King of Egypt and the Princess Amneris came to meet their General and watched the great procession, and Aida also watched, because she was the Princess's slave. The King said that Radames should now marry the Princess as a reward for his victory over the Ethiopians. The people of Egypt were very happy.

In the procession of prisoners, Aida saw her own father, who had not been killed in the battle and was pretending to be an ordinary soldier. She called out to her father but he told her quietly not to tell anyone that he was the King as the Egyptians would kill him if they knew. Radames decided to allow all the prisoners to go home except for Aida and her father.

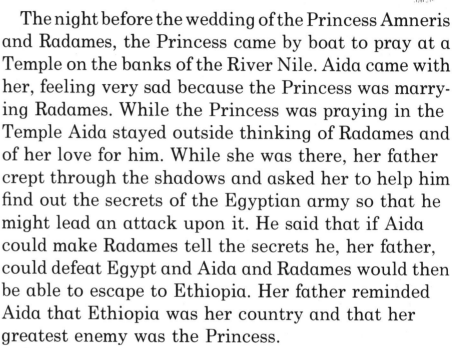

The night before the wedding of the Princess Amneris and Radames, the Princess came by boat to pray at a Temple on the banks of the River Nile. Aida came with her, feeling very sad because the Princess was marrying Radames. While the Princess was praying in the Temple Aida stayed outside thinking of Radames and of her love for him. While she was there, her father crept through the shadows and asked her to help him find out the secrets of the Egyptian army so that he might lead an attack upon it. He said that if Aida could make Radames tell the secrets he, her father, could defeat Egypt and Aida and Radames would then be able to escape to Ethiopia. Her father reminded Aida that Ethiopia was her country and that her greatest enemy was the Princess.

At last Aida agreed and when Radames arrived at the Temple she found out from him the secrets her father wanted. But everything they said to each other was overheard by the Princess and she ordered soldiers to capture them. Aida and her father escaped but Radames surrendered to the soldiers and was taken back to the city as a prisoner.

Radames was taken to the Judges who ordered that he must die as a traitor and be buried alive underneath the great Temple in the city. He was taken down into the room and a great stone was placed over the entrance. The room was very dark and even the brave Radames felt very frightened. But when he called out Aida's name there was a movement in a corner of the room and from out of the darkness came Aida. She had hidden herself in the room before Radames was led down there so that she could die with him. And so they stayed together until the end.

About the music

Aida is an opera. An opera is a play set to music. It is performed on a stage and the singers act as well as sing. This opera was written by Verdi, an Italian composer, who lived just over one hundred years ago.

The opera was written in Italian, though it is often performed in English. It lasts about two and a half hours and is full of beautiful songs and exciting music. The opera is divided into four main parts called 'acts' and all the acts, except Act 3, have two scenes. These show the palaces and temples of ancient Egypt with statues of the kings and the gods of that country. The second scene of Act 2 shows the great gate of the old capital city of Egypt called Thebes. It is here that the King and the Princess Amneris come to meet General Radames to celebrate his great victory over the army of Aida's father, the King of Ethiopia. There is a great procession of soldiers, dancers and prisoners.

Act 2 – Scene 2 A gate in the city of Thebes

At the front of the stage is a group of palm trees. To the right is the temple of the god Ammon. To the left is a throne for the King and the Princess Amneris. At the back of the stage is the gate. The scene is crowded with people.

Trumpets sound and the King enters followed by his ministers, priests, captains and slaves carrying huge fans made of feathers. Then the Princess enters with Aida and her slave girls. The King sits on the throne with Princess Amneris beside him. Aida stands at the side.

The people watching the procession first sing of the glory of Egypt, the goddess Isis and their King (*gloria* is Italian for 'glory'). Then the women sing that they will weave a crown of flowers for General Radames and dance special dances in honour of the gods. Next the priests sing, telling the people to worship the gods who have brought the victory.

The trumpets and orchestra play a march and a procession of Egyptian soldiers moves across the stage in front of the King. After the marching soldiers come battle chariots and then statues of the gods are carried in by more soldiers. Next the music changes to a dance and girls carry in treasure captured from the enemy. The whole stage is a mass of excitement as the grand procession passes in front of the King and through the gates of the city. At last, General Radames is carried in on a chair held by four soldiers. As he enters, the dancing stops and the Egyptian people sing a song of welcome while the priests call upon them again to worship the gods who have brought the victory.

● Choose one person for Princess Amneris and another for the King, her father. The rest, divide into four groups:
Group 1 to be priests;
Group 2 to be soldiers;
Group 3 to be women; and
Group 4 to be slave girls.

Listen to the music again.
Group 1 enter to the music carrying fans;
Group 2 march like soldiers;
Group 3 enter carrying treasure captured from the enemy;
Group 4 slave girls group round Aida, who is sitting on a throne next to her father.

Next time the music is played, all groups can change round. The 'Things to do and make' section tells you how to make masks and fans to help you act the story.

It is always fun to march to a rousing tune. Here is
some music you are sure to enjoy.

Oh, the grand old Duke of York

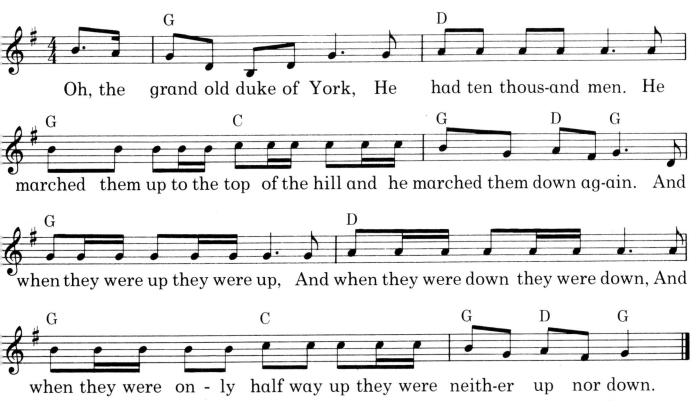

Oh, the grand old duke of York, He had ten thous-and men. He
marched them up to the top of the hill and he marched them down ag-ain. And
when they were up they were up, And when they were down they were down, And
when they were on - ly half way up they were neith-er up nor down.

● It is great fun to bang the empty shells of a coconut
together. This will make the sound of horses'
hooves. Try to make these shells clap in time to the
music of *The grand old Duke of York*.

● Now read this poem. You could say it all together and make it sound as if you were marching in a ceremonial band.

The ceremonial band

The old King of Dorchester,
He had a little orchestra,
And never did you hear such
        a ceremonial band.
'Tootle-too,' said the flute,
'Deed-a-reedle,' said the fiddle,
For the fiddles and the flutes were
        the finest in the land.

The old King of Dorchester,
He had a little orchestra,
And never did you hear such
        a ceremonial band.
'Pump-a-rum,' said the drum,
'Tootle-too,' said the flute,
'Deed-a-reedle,' said the fiddle,
For the fiddles and flutes were
        the finest in the land.

The old King of Dorchester,
He had a little orchestra,
And never did you hear such
        a ceremonial band.
'Pah-pa-rah,' said the trumpet,
'Pump-a-rum,' said the drum,
'Tootle-too,' said the flute,
'Deed-a-reedle,' said the fiddle,
For the fiddles and flutes were
        the finest in the land.

The old King of Dorchester,
He had a little orchestra,
And never did you hear such
        a ceremonial band.
'Pickle-pee,' said the fife,
'Pah-pa-rah,' said the trumpet,
'Pump-a-rum,' said the drum,
'Tootle-too,' said the flute,
'Deed-a-reedle,' said the fiddle,
For the fiddles and the flutes were
        the finest in the land.

The old King of Dorchester,
He had a little orchestra,
And never did you hear such
        a ceremonial band.
'Zoomba-zoom,' said the bass,
'Pickle-pee,' said the fife,
'Pah-pa-rah,' said the trumpet,
'Pump-a-rum,' said the drum,
'Tootle-too,' said the flute,
'Deed-a-reedle,' said the fiddle,
For the fiddles and the flutes were
        the finest in the land.

JAMES REEVES

Things to do and make

When you are listening to the music of *Aida*, it will be more fun if you act the characters. First you need to make six palm trees.

Palm trees

You will need

6 sheets of newspaper

sticky tape

scissors

1 Roll up a sheet of newspaper.

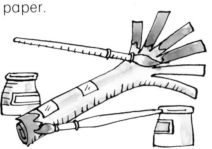

2 Cut one end carefully into strips.

3 Now fasten the trunk with a piece of sticky tape.

4 Now paint the trunk brown, and the leaves green.

5 Make six trees to hold while the music is being played.

Fan

Behind the throne of the King and Princess Amneris, two slaves should stand. They could gently fan the Royal pair.

You will need

2 sheets of newspaper

glue

scissors

2 canes

paint

1 Cut strips along the newspaper for about three-quarters of the sheet.

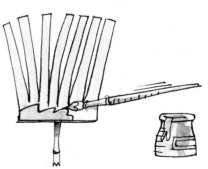

2 Now glue the uncut piece on to the cane. Paint the fan in a bright colour.

Trumpet

Soldiers playing trumpets lead the procession.

You will need

a sheet of plain white paper

sticky tape

paint

1 Roll your sheet of paper into a cone shape.

2 Fasten the end with sticky tape and paint it yellow.

Masks

When you act the characters, it would be more 'real' to wear masks like the ones in the pictures.

You will need

4 outline masks drawn by your teacher or an adult

paints or felt-tipped pens

1 Cut out the masks and colour them. Felt-tipped pens show up well.

2 The King and General Radames. They would wear many rich jewels and probably a long skirt. Egypt is a very hot country, so men would not wear anything on the top half of their bodies.

3 Princess Amneris. She was the beautiful daughter of the King of Egypt and would probably wear a flower in her hair, and many necklaces and bracelets.

4 Aida and the other slave girls, who waited on the Princess and her friends. They brushed and dressed the Princess's hair, and helped her dress.

5 The soldiers, who would carry spears, bow and arrows and shields. There were many wars in Egypt and every man, including the Pharaoh, the ruler of Egypt, went to fight.

An Egyptian war chariot

Many of the Egyptian soldiers rode in chariots to battle and some of them bought their own chariots. These chariots were strong, yet light, and were made of wood, but the bindings were of leather.

Make your own Egyptian war chariot.

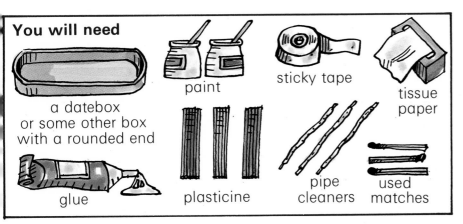

You will need

paint

sticky tape

tissue paper

a datebox or some other box with a rounded end

glue

plasticine

pipe cleaners

used matches

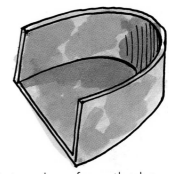

1 Cut a piece from the box, about 5 cm.

2 Now fix a pipe cleaner for the shaft.

3 Now make a pipe cleaner into a circle.

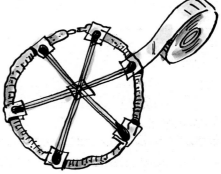

4 Fix six used matches for spokes using sticky tape.

5 Fix with a blob of plasticine to a pipe cleaner. Make another wheel, and fix on the other end.

6 Now glue your axle to the bottom of the chariot.

7 Paint your chariot carefully.

Horse

The Egyptian war chariot would need a horse to pull it.

You will need
Clay, dough or plasticine

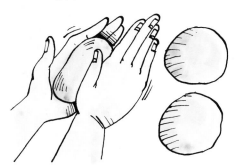

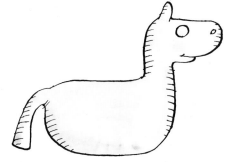

1 Roll your lump of clay in your hand until it is soft and easy to work. Divide into two.

2 Shape the head and body. Remember the ears and the tail.

3 With the second piece of clay, make four legs. Mould them on to the body.

Soldier

You could make a soldier to ride in your chariot.

You will need
3 pipe cleaners   1 bead

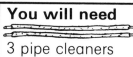

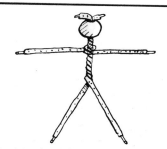

1 Thread two pipe cleaners through the bead for 1 cm. Bend the ends over the bead.

2 Twist the pipe cleaners four times for the body and divide the rest for the legs.

3 Twist the third pipe cleaner round the body twice and bend the ends to make arms.

Bow and arrow

Give your soldier a bow and arrow.

You will need
string
tissue paper
clay   1 pipe cleaner cut in half

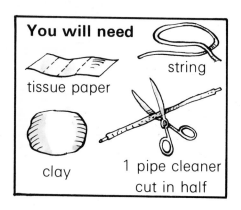

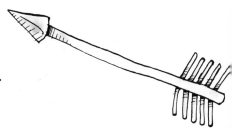

1 Tie a small piece of string to one end of a half pipe cleaner. Now bend the pipe cleaner slightly and tie the string to the other end.

2 Use the other half pipe cleaner for the arrow. Make the head with a piece of clay and the (feathery) end with some strips of tissue paper.

Now your soldier is ready for battle. He has his bow and arrow, his war chariot and his horse.

HANSEL AND GRETEL

In a cottage on the edge of a dark forest in Germany, there once lived a family of broom-makers. There was a father called Peter, a mother called Gertrud, and their two children, a boy called Hansel and a girl called Gretel. They were all very poor and lived by cutting twigs and small branches from the trees growing at the edge of the forest and then binding them together to make brooms. Peter and Gertrud would try to sell the brooms in the villages near where they lived. When people needed new brooms they would pay Peter and Gertrud a few pennies with which food could be bought.

One day, while both their parents were out trying to sell their brooms, Hansel and Gretel were left alone in the cottage. Hansel had been told to bind more twigs into brooms and Gretel was sitting knitting stockings. They were both very hungry for there had been hardly any food to eat for days.

Gretel tried to cheer up her brother by telling him of a beautiful jug of milk which a kind neighbour had brought to them that morning. But Hansel was impatient for his food and instead of working, asked Gretel to teach him to dance. Round and round they danced, tapping their feet and clapping their hands, forgetting that they were hungry until suddenly the door opened and their mother came home.

Now Gertrud was very tired and very unhappy. She had sold no brooms that day and had no food to give the children. She became angry with them because they were dancing and in her anger she knocked over the jug and the beautiful milk spilt all over the floor. Now there was no food at all and she shouted at the children, telling them to go out and look for strawberries and not to come back until their basket was full.

After a long time, Peter came home to the cottage. He sang as he came home because he had sold all his brooms. When he heard that Hansel and Gretel had gone into the forest to look for strawberries, he became very worried.

It was getting dark and he told Gertrud of the stories of the Nibblewitch who lived there and who tempted children into her home with her magic cakes. Once they were inside, she would pop them into her oven and turn them into gingerbread for her to eat. Peter and Gertrud rushed out of the house to look for Hansel and Gretel, not noticing that far overhead the Nibblewitch was riding her broomstick searching for her food.

Meanwhile in the wood Hansel and Gretel filled their basket with some beautiful strawberries. They were happy and forgot how late it was until suddenly it began to get dark.

Now this forest was an enchanted forest and as darkness came the trees began to whisper and from their trunks faces peered at the children. A mist crept between the trees and strange lights flickered here and

there. Voices called and Hansel and Gretel were very frightened.

Suddenly the mist parted and a little man came towards them. He was the Sandman who loves all children and quietens them before they sleep. He sang gently to Hansel and Gretel and they settled down to sleep among the leaves. Instead of the evil faces, 14 angels guarded the children all night until morning came.

When Hansel and Gretel awoke the mists lifted and to their surprise, there was a little house made all of sugar, cakes and sweets, and surrounded by rows of gingerbread men.

The children were very hungry and the little house looked very tempting. They ran towards it and Hansel broke off a small piece of cake from one of the corners. As he did so, a strange voice came from the house: 'Nibble, nibble nousey, who's nibbling at my housey?' Hansel dropped the cake. But soon they were nibbling again, and again came the voice.

Now as you will have guessed, this beautiful house made of sweets and cakes was really the house of the wicked Nibblewitch. She seized the children and immediately shut Hansel in a magic cage so that she could fatten him up to eat. But Gretel she allowed to work in the house and lay the table for her feast. This was a mistake because Gretel was a clever girl.

The Witch was so pleased at having caught the children that she jumped on to her broomstick and rode around the cottage. Gretel watched her carefully and noticed all she did. She noticed how the Witch cast her spells and how she broke them again. She remembered all this and while the Witch was lighting the oven, Gretel repeated a spell and freed Hansel from the cage.

The Witch then told Gretel to look inside the oven to see how the gingerbread biscuits were cooking. She thought Gretel looked fat enough to eat and that it was time to push her into the oven. But Gretel was a clever girl and asked first to be shown what she should do. The Witch thought her stupid and began to peer into the oven. This was her second mistake. Hansel and Gretel together gave her a good push sending her flying inside and then slammed the door behind her.

The oven roared and crackled, flames shot out in all directions. Then there was a bang and the oven exploded with the Witch inside.

Hansel and Gretel stood still, very frightened. Suddenly, there in front of them, instead of rows of gingerbread men, were children enchanted by the Nibblewitch. Hansel and Gretel broke the spells which bound the children. They woke as if from a deep sleep and began to dance round singing their thanks to Hansel and Gretel.

As they sang and danced together a new sound was heard in the forest as Peter and Gertrud came through the trees looking for their children. So Peter and Gertrud found Hansel and Gretel again and as some of the children danced round them, others pulled from the remains of the oven the Witch who had now been turned into gingerbread.

About the music

The opera *Hansel and Gretel* was composed by Engelbert Humperdinck, who was born in Germany in 1854 and died in 1921. The words were written by the composer's sister, who based them on the fairy story by the Brothers Grimm.

The story of the opera is about the power of good overcoming evil and Humperdinck uses the music to the story and to tell us more about each of the characters.

In the cottage, Gretel teaches Hansel to dance.

● Find a partner and dance to Gretel's song. Here are the words. Read them and sing while you dance.

Brother, come and dance with me,
Both my hands, I offer thee,
Right foot first, left foot then,
Round about and back again!

With your foot, you tap, tap, tap,
With your hands, you clap, clap, clap,
Right foot first, left foot then,
Round about and back again!

With your head, you nick, nick, nick,
With your fingers, you click, click, click,
Right foot first, left foot then,
Round about and back again!

The prayer theme

A theme is another word for a tune. Humperdinck has a special theme to show when the powers of good are protecting the children. You can hear it first at the beginning of the overture, which is the music which begins the opera before the curtain rises and the action begins. You will hear it again in the wood for just as Gretel runs screaming from the misty faces which crowd round her, suddenly they part and the little

Sandman appears with his sack on his back. He soothes the children and they kneel to say their prayers.

● Hear the prayer theme again as they sing:

When at night I go to sleep,
Fourteen angels watch do keep.
Two my head are guarding,
Two my feet are guiding,
Two are on my right hand,
Two are on my left hand,
Two who warmly cover,
Two who round me hover,
Two to whom 'tis given
To guide my steps to heaven.

The Witch

Humperdinck contrasts the prayer theme with the music given to the Witch who represents the evil forces which try to destroy the children. Her music is jerky and sounds as if it has sharp corners. It is often played by the oboe which you will not hear nearly as much in the 'good' music of the prayer theme.

● Listen in particular for the Witch's spell:

'Hocus pocus, bonus jocus,
Malus locus, hocus pocus,
Bonus locus, malus locus.'

● Now make up your own spell. Pretend to be a witch and chant a spell while you ride your broomstick over the forest.

The Brothers Grimm

The story of Hansel and Gretel was one of many collected by Jacob and Wilhelm Grimm, nearly two hundred years ago.

Jacob was born in 1785 and Wilhelm in 1786, and they always did everything together. When they were young, the brothers listened to as many stories and legends as they could, and wrote them down. Some were very frightening, some were exciting, and some had happy endings. These fairy tales came from many countries and have been translated into many languages.

Hansel and Gretel, as you have read, was made into an opera by the composer, Engelbert Humperdinck, and Walt Disney made a film about Snow White and the Seven Dwarfs, and Cinderella. Other well-known tales are *Snow White and Rose Red*, *Rumpelstiltskin*, *The Elves and the Shoemaker*, *The Goose Girl*, and *The Musicians of Bremen*.

At Christmas time, *Cinderella*, *The Sleeping Beauty*, and *Red Riding Hood* are made into pantomimes. *The Sleeping Beauty* has also been danced as a ballet at Covent Garden with music by a famous composer named Tchaikovsky.

The musicians of Bremen

In a village near Bremen in Germany, there lived a man and a donkey. The donkey had worked for many years and was very old. He thought the man would sell him so he ran away.

The donkey loved music, and so he decided to go to Bremen and join the town band. Soon the donkey saw a dog lying by the road. The dog told him that his master was going to kill him because he was too old to hunt. So the donkey and the dog decided to go to Bremen together.

Soon the donkey and the dog met a cat. She was very sad because she was old and could not catch mice for her mistress. The cat thought her mistress would drown her, so she decided to go to Bremen to become a town musician.

Soon the donkey, the dog and the cat met a cock. The cock was crowing as loudly as he could. He told the animals that his mistress was planning to make him into soup on the following day, so he was singing loudly while he could. The donkey asked the cock to join the animals and become a musician in the town band. So now there were four animals walking along the road to Bremen.

When night came, the animals chose a tree in the forest where they could spend the night. The donkey and the dog lay under the tree, the cat sat on a branch and the cock flew to the very top of the tree. From this high position he saw a light in the distance and called out that there must be a house there. So the four friends walked towards the light. Gradually it became larger and brighter, and soon they reached the house.

The donkey looked through the window and saw some robbers sitting round a table. They had good food and drink and were enjoying themselves. The four animals were very hungry and decided to frighten the robbers away.

Very quietly, the dog jumped on the donkey's back. Then the cat got onto the dog. Lastly the cock flew onto the back of the cat. The donkey nodded his head and all the animals began to sing. It was a dreadful noise. The donkey braying, the dog barking, the cat miaowing, and the cock crowing. Then they jumped through the window and the terrified robbers ran out through the door into the forest.

The animals were very hungry so they ate a big supper with plenty of food and drink. Then they turned off the light and looked for a place to sleep. The donkey found some straw in the yard. The dog found a blanket behind the door. The cat curled up on a rug by the fire. The cock flew up to the ceiling and settled on a beam.

While the animals slept, the robbers watched from the forest. They saw the light go out in the house and they planned to send one robber back to the house. This robber went quietly back to the house and went inside. He saw the bright eyes of the cat and thought they were a light. He put his candle near the cat but she jumped at the man, spitting and scratching. The robber ran to the door and fell over the dog. The dog jumped up and bit the leg of the man. The robber ran across the yard and the donkey kicked him hard. Then the cock flew screeching down from his beam.

The robber was very frightened and limped back to his friends in the forest. He told the other robbers that he had met a witch in the house. She had scratched his face with her claws. Then, by the door, a man with a sharp knife had stabbed his leg. Outside in the yard, a monster with a wooden stick had beaten him, while a judge had shouted from the roof that the robbers should be caught.

When the robbers heard this dreadful story they said they would never go near the house again.

The four friends lived in the house and were very happy, but they never went to Bremen to join the town band.

● Here is a map of Germany. Look at it carefully and you will see Bremen where the donkey, the dog, the cat, and the cock all planned to go to become town musicians.

Look also for the Reinhardswald, the forest of the Sleeping Beauty, and her castle at Sababurg. Can you find Kassel where there is a museum of the Brothers Grimm, and the Harz Mountains where the witches ride? The Gingerbread House may be found near the city of Hamburg.

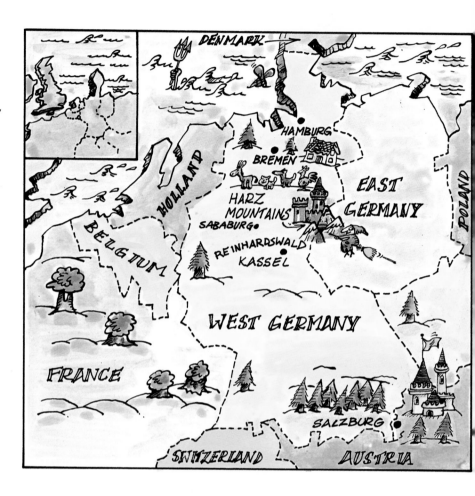

About witches

Hallowe'en is on October 31st. It is the eve of, or day before, the Feast of All Saints.

At Hallowe'en all the witches are said to ride on their broomsticks across the sky. Here is a poem about the witches at Hallowe'en.

Hallowe'en

This is the night when witches fly,
On their whizzing broomsticks through the wintry sky;
Steering up the pathway where the stars are strewn,
They stretch skinny fingers to the waking moon.

LEONARD CLARK

● Make up your own poem about a witch.

44

Things to do and make

Gingerbread house

Now you can make a Gingerbread house.

You will need

a cardboard box

a piece of thin card

old magazines

paints or felt-tips

sticky tape or glue

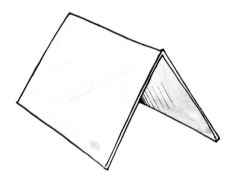

1 Bend the piece of card in half to make a roof shape.

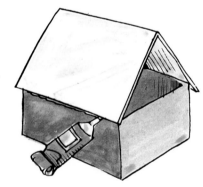

2 Glue the roof on to your box.

3 Draw a door and windows with paints or felt-tips.

4 Decorate your house. Cut out pictures of sweets and chocolates from magazines. Advertisements for Smarties are good.

5 Glue them on to your Gingerbread house.

6 If you cannot find any pictures to cut out, you could draw and paint your own sweets to make the house look lovely to eat.

Now you have read the story of Hansel and Gretel, you will want to make your own characters to act the story.

You will need

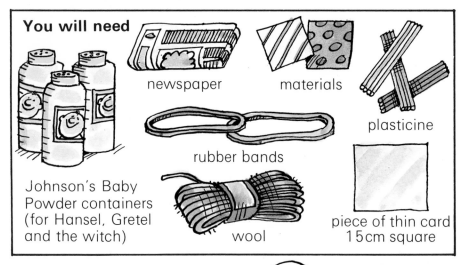

Johnson's Baby Powder containers (for Hansel, Gretel and the witch)

newspaper

materials

plasticine

rubber bands

wool

piece of thin card 15 cm square

Hansel

1 Remove lid from Johnson's Baby Powder container.

2 Roll a sheet of newspaper into a ball and put a rubber band round the ends. The picture shows you how this will make the neck.

3 Cover newspaper head with a light-coloured material. Fix the head into the neck of the powder container.

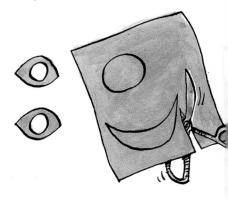

4 Cut out two eyes, a nose and a mouth.

5 Glue on some wool for hair.

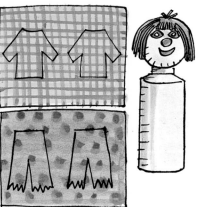

6 Now cut out some trousers and a shirt and glue the clothes on the body.

7 Cut out some hands and glue them on to the arms. Now your Hansel is ready.

Gretel

1 Glue longer strips of wool for her hair.

2 Instead of trousers, make a dress for her. Cut two pieces of material like the one in the diagram and glue the dress on to the body.

3 Cut out two hands and glue them on to the sleeves.

The Witch

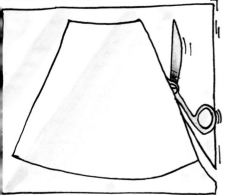

1 Make a long cloak for her out of black material.

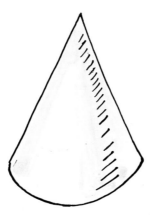

2 Give her a tall pointed hat made of cardboard.

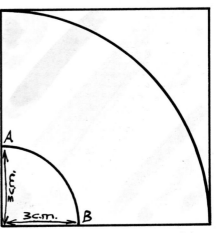

3 Measure 3cm on two sides of the card. Cut from A to B. Ask an adult to help you cut an arc from C to D.

4 Roll your paper into a cone. Glue carefully.

5 Paint your witch's hat black. Glue on to her head.

6 Make her a pointed nose out of dough or plasticine.

Gingerbread children

All round the Witch's house were children made of gingerbread.

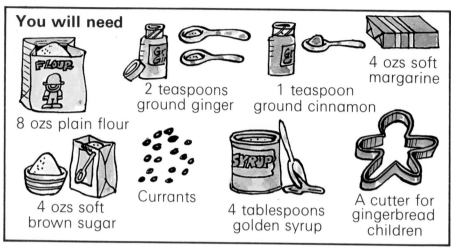

You will need

8 ozs plain flour

2 teaspoons ground ginger

1 teaspoon ground cinnamon

4 ozs soft margarine

4 ozs soft brown sugar

Currants

4 tablespoons golden syrup

A cutter for gingerbread children

1 Sift together the flour, ginger and cinnamon.

2 Put the margarine, brown sugar and golden syrup into a saucepan. Place on a low heat and stir gently until melted.

3 Pour into the flour mixture and mix to a dough.

4 Turn onto a floured board and roll out.

5 Use the cutter to make the children's shapes.

6 Use two currants for eyes, one for nose and one for mouth. You might want to use currants for buttons.

7 Put in the centre of a moderate oven (Gas 5 or 350°F) for 10–12 minutes until brown. Remove from oven and allow to cool.